ALLIES

by
Robert J. Shapiro and Edouard Mabe

Edited by Allyn B. Brodsky

Illustrations by Fu-Ding Cheng

Cover: Pleiadian Landscape.

Copyright © 1983 by
Robert J. Shapiro and Edouard Mabe

We wish to acknowledge the following people who have contributed their time, help, support and love to this project;

> Sylvia Barnes
> Allyn B. Brodsky
> Michael Chadwick
> Fu Ding Cheng
> Jim Chu
> Larry Doran
> Terry Gwiazdowski
> Robin Haas
> Sherman Kang
> Karen Lehrer
>
> Sara Self
> Lorraine Shapiro
> Glenn Williams

Dedicated to our readers, who will be the future founders of our planet.

--R. J. S. and E. M.

EDITOR'S NOTE

While telepathic mediumship makes it possible for us to communicate directly with off-planet beings, there remain certain difficulties in the presentation in book form of the communications received. These representatives of interstellar civilizations are attempting to explain concepts and structures of their cultures through the use of colloquial, present-day English. Their vital personalities and energetic style do much to assist communication in live discussion, or even on tape.

However, we have chosen not to attempt to rephrase or alter the transcripts of those conversations for a written format. The sole editing done was to group messages from representatives of the same civilization and to collect questions on related topics.

Where directed by the off-planet beings themselves, certain information has been reserved for future volumes.

INTRODUCTION BY SAMUEL

(Samuel is a non-physical energy personality who speaks through Robert)

Now is the beginning of mankind's evolution toward a conscious understanding of his development. There is an inkling, you might say, a pinpoint of light. You may call that light understanding. But ongoing efforts will be toward survival.

There will be issues which will confuse, cause doubts. In the final analysis these doubts will seem petty, silly. But for you, at your now stage of understanding, in order to communicate fully with those off-planet beings you will really have to consider allowing that pinpoint of light called understanding to develop into the size which will accommodate your entire spatial frame. That frame that you use as a reference between your now understanding of yourself and your coming understanding.

For it is really up to you who read this book to know it is not just a book, but really a method you have, on your own, utilized to activate your unconscious recollection of events which have preceeded your now conviction to the ideas that you are not alone on this planet. That you are really only beginning to uncover the mysteries of your universe. You will then be willing to go forward.

As you go through the pages, let each one unfurl slowly in front of you. Allow memories and imaginations to permeate these words, so that they become visualizations and ideas for you. Allow an understanding to come into your now way of life so that you will be receptive, in time, to true physical contact with those off-planet beings. When you are ready, when you have maintained a balance of loving integrity within you, then and only then will you be ready to share true love and understanding with another.

Those off-planet beings will not approach you with defense systems, nor will they approach you for physical contact with offense systems. They will only approach you with love.

So for your part, you have only to reciprocate in kind and begin to love yourself. When you do so, when you truly accomplish this worthy deed, then and only then can you share your love with those who will come to meet and greet you.

As you are reading through this book, understand that for you then this is really a tool you have manifested for your use. Don't, if you will, think about it as casual reading. These are really love letters from your off-planet brethren. Love letters to you from beings who care about you, who love you and who are looking forward to being with you in harmony.

So it is then, that as you come to the end of this volume, be willing to write volumes of your own in your experience with yourself. Be willing to imagine beautiful off-planet places that you would like to visit. Be willing to imagine that with their assistance, the off-planet beings, you can, if you wish, rebuild your own planet into just as beautiful a place.

They will bring you only gifts of love and harmony, and you will in time truly realize that what you have here before you is a loving image, and they will be created in your image as you are created in theirs. For it is a harmony of body as well as spirit. So for you, let this book be an opening chapter in your life. Let it truly activate your own love consciousness.

The Activation Process

This is a process in thought, a method of communicating in tone and electrical energy, a telepathic form of imparting potential creative forces to you and through you, to allow you to recall what it is you came here to do.

Your activation then is something that you do. You activate yourself by discovering your own purpose. All activation is done this way and is not the result of outside forces.

Many times activation will take place on its own, in its own time and way, always with the comfort of the individual. But there are those occasions when certain individuals choose to experience this activation through contact with spiritual or other forms of consciousness than their own--an energy stimulation to become what you will become in any event.

Sometimes this is an attempt to increase speed, a way of decreasing the time between when you had intended to start working toward your job. You may wish to receive an outside stimulation to work toward your job sooner. The reception by you of this outside stimulation will help you on the conscious level to believe in what you are doing. It is really a method you manifest for yourself in order to know that there are other forces than the energies you meet in your daily life.

--Samuel

PREFACE

Like myself, I am sure that many of our readers have had little difficulty in accepting the concept of extraterrestrial life. What has been missing is a dialog with those off-planet beings that we have come to refer to as "aliens."

Who are they? Where are they from? Why are they here? These are the questions I had asked myself. And now, I hope to begin providing the answers, directly from the source.

Let us begin to look at what they have to say for themselves. We take for granted the idea that these beings are more aware of their abilities than we are. I want to provide here some background on the methods of communication used, for a better understanding of how these communications take place.

We have all heard popular notions of what has commonly been referred to as "extra-sensory perception" (ESP). Maybe you have also had experiences of your own of this nature. Clearly, telepathy is an idea whose time has come.

These beings that inhabit the universe, these "aliens" --or, more appropriately, "allies," for they are indeed here not as threatening others but as loving friends who wish to help--have fully developed telepathy as their primary means of communication, not only between themselves but also for what we would call interplanetary communication as well.

Telepathy knows no time or space limitations such as those which seem to govern our current means to be in contact with one another. Telepathy allows for a free flow and exchange of information and feeling, regardless of the location of those involved in the exchange.

Feeling is the key word here because this is the heart

of the telepathic exchange. Not only is an idea exchanged but more important, the feeling behind the thought is also transmitted. This results in much clearer and more meaningful exchange between beings, whether they are of the same world or vastly different ones.

These telepathic abilities are as much a part of our world as they are of the worlds of our allies, but until now, we on this planet have chosen not really to develop these means. We all have, latent within us, many abilities that we do not develop to their fullest potential. But consider for a moment that maybe you have been using these methods without knowing it. Indeed, this is the case with most of us.

Transcribed information within this book was transmitted to us telepathically from our allies. Initial telepathic contact with off-planet beings assisted in the development of Robert's abilities as a medium, and his improved mediumship then allowed for the direct channeling of information. It also provided and opportunity for an exchange of ideas and information. I was able to ask direct questions and engage in conversation, as we think of it, with the off-planet beings as they spoke through Robert.

This form of communication--telepathic mediumship-- is as commonplace and "normal" for our allies as picking up the telephone to speak with someone on the other side of the planet is for us; it simply eliminates the need for the physical instruments involved.

Over many hours of this form of contact I felt as if I began to get to know the beings we were speaking with. They, just as we on this planet, have their own unique personalities. Repeatedly they stressed the common bonds between us, how very much alike we are. Many of them are physical beings who appear quite close to what we think of as "human," and as we proceed, we will discover many more common links between them and ourselves.

The allies encourage us to learn about ourselves, to get in touch with our own being, our own uniqueness. They have much to offer this planet, if only we are willing to listen with an open mind and heart. Some of them have experienced situations on their own planets in their past similar to those we face here presently. They have an understanding of why things on this planet appear to be as they are, and ways to change and improve the quality of life here.

They have absolutely no desire or intent to interfere in any way with life on this planet. It is not in their interests to disrupt life here, as would happen if they were to suddenly land in every backyard and on every street corner.

But they are willing and ready to share the knowledge of their existence with the masses on our planet, and then to work with us as we wish, toward our own goals and ambitions. It is up to us to take responsibility for ourselves and our own future, as well as the future of our planet. They are willing, even anxious, to assist us in any way we desire as we set out to create a better world for ourselves.

--Edouard

WHY ARE THEY HERE?

"Why are they here?" is a question often at the root of everyone's current concern about the presence of our allies.

For too long we allowed ourselves to believe that they were here, in one way or another, to colonize or conquer our planet. This simply is not true.

The allies are here out of love for our planet and universe. As a result of, as we see it, their greater knowledge, they have a broader understanding of the state of life as it exists on our planet. Many of them have had experiences similar to ours on their own planets, or are aware of the existence of negativity in other forms.

They are here to offer us the benefits of their experience, so that we can utilize this to form new ideas for ourselves on this planet. They understand peace and can help us achieve it for ourselves.

The allies also want us to know we are not alone on this planet, that life exists throughout the universe as we think of it and that we can reap the benefits of this awareness.

The following communications were among the initial contacts, and provide general background about why they are here as well as advice to us about benefiting from their presence.

The first is from a representative of an advanced culture centered at Alpha Centauri, the nearest star to our sun. The ambassador, Zoosh, is a non-physical being although the Alpha Centauri System also includes physical planets and beings. His culture is one which is devoted to pure thought and knowledge.

The second communication is from a representative of a civilization located within Jupiter, the fifth planet of our sun. Our recent scientific space probes have not detected traces of this civilization.

Both contacts responded to the initial question, "Why are you here?"

AN AMBASSADOR FROM ALPHA CENTAURI

You are proceeding in your reality as we are in ours. It is our intention to assist you in re-creating your world within your own positive image. We know of the work you are doing.

We have our own network of planets and galaxies. It is for you now to establish your network of individuals who are willing to assist in your project and by so doing you will set up the initial belief systems which will function as co-ordinating points within your now planet to utilize individual thought patterns.

Your speech syntax is foreign to me, but even with my limited abilities I would struggle through a "thank you," for it is that though you are pursuing what you must do for yourselves, you are also creating a service for all other individuals, from my galaxy and others, as we all observe you. So it is that we wish you good cheer in your efforts and will abide them well.

We seek to assist you when you are ready, and perform some small functions for you now, though most of you are unaware.

I would say again thank you for your assistance in our project and yours, and welcome you to our network, which has its origin in Seat of Thought in Alpha Centauri.

So I bid you good experience.

--Zoosh

REPRESENTATIVE FROM JUPITER

A love of life and intellectual pursuits can be had if you are willing to create it. Sing your song of creation and develop your own lives to your own tune. Perceive what you wish to create in your minds' eye and simply create it. It is really not so difficult, one perceives what one needs. Establish your need within your own universe by merely speaking it aloud upon rising. Your universe can be changed merely by changing your thoughts, and eventually your belief will change also. Is it such a difficult proposal? Only a change of mind.

You might say, you philosophers, that a change of heart and soul is involved, but really the change we are talking about here is a change of thought--for it is thought which is the creator of all that exists everywhere and every time in every space. Pure thought exists in all forms and realities. Pure thought exists before all else, regardless of shape of type of existence, and it is the purity of thought which can create all that you wish to create. A discipline of the mind; that is what is necessary. You might say a grounding of negative energies.

Concentrate. Focus your mind completely on the purity of your thoughts. As a training technique, you might try to focus totally on one particular thought for just thirty seconds, completely excluding all other conscious thoughts. This technique will allow you to express a greater interest in what it is you wish to develop. When you are ready, when you feel you can create pure thought for ten seconds, upon rising place your need in the universe for a more positive world, and keep your thought completely pure while placing this need within your intellectual, emotional, and vibrational atmosphere.

This type of technique will reach out and touch all forms of consciousness, and will help to re-create the world in the image of positivity, if you wish it.

Jupiterian Logic suggests that this technique is considerably more powerful than many who tried in the past of your time have been told.

Re-creation of thought must begin with creation of need. The world of the future is yours to create now. We have created our own world where literally nothing but ashes once stood in its place. A world beyond your world knows what can be done if one is willing to practice and apply what you really know, this being the knowledge of your full and total self. The pureness and the willingness to re-create totally that which exists in a negative form in a different probability. For what do you have but more than one path to follow? You will choose your own path.

We are here to assist you if you wish it, but remember you will choose your own path. So it has been and so it must be. Our assistance is available to you and we are very willing to be a part of your positive future. We believe you will choose this type of future, and I can assure you that many of the others who are in your area on other craft hold out for that eventual, probable, positive future for your planet.

It is true that some are here to observe only, but most are here to assist you in any way you will allow. Since mediumship contact is what you are willing to allow at this point, then that is what we will assist you with.

Bring the world home with you, my friends, and re-create the new one to exist. We shall see, all of us, the joy of the new world, and it will be the joy of my compadres, as you might say, within the area on other craft, and those on the other worlds who are watching. It will be our joy and yours to see the re-birth of an entire planet into the more positive world of the future. Sing your song of re-creation and the chorus will be played by your brothers on other planets.

THE PLEIADES

A cluster of young, bright stars located about 400 light years from Earth, the Pleiades System has developed a rich culture known thoughout the universe for its joy, love and harmony. Pleiadians are among the beings most like us, and it is thought that the Pleiadian culture is closest in harmony with what we on Earth could develop, if we choose.

Our contact from the Pleiades is named Ptaah and has a lively and joyful personality. In the following material, Ptaah shares with us many facets of the beautiful lifestyle on his planet.

You know, on our planet we do believe in happiness and joy, and express this through a great deal of laughter, an idea which is rapidly coming into its own on your planet. Laughter is good for the soul you know, when you do it you feel so good. Well, we also on our planet. We encourage this laughter, not through jokes as you understand them but what you might call community laughter and joviality. We encourage happiness, as you have noticed by listening to the dialogs which I have provided you with, and there is a preponderance of joy which cycles through the planet and all the inhabitants upon our system, the planetary system that we call our home.

I would encourage you to ask me questions and I will provide you with that information which you feel you require at this time. You may feel free to use this material in any book as you should so wish.

Now I will just interject some comments on why we are here. We are here to assist your planet in your natural evolution toward a positive future. We see our mission as one to assist our brothers, those who are very much like us in thought and deed, into the positive side.

We have had the opportunity to experience our positive evolution, an experience which you have not chosen to do for the past few thousands of your years. But there is no reason for you not to do so in the future, and when you do decide to live in your positive future we shall do what we can to catch you up, so to speak, as you will wish to take advantage of a lifestyle which we have experimented with and which we will utilize. You might wish to take advantage of some of our spiritual insights, or technological know-how. We will be pleased to provide you with that information, and to encourage your spiritual growth on your own. We feel comfortable with you as human beings. We are, as you understand it, also human beings, and feel that you will be comfortable with us also. Question?

Question: In many ways it seems that what we see on this planet as positive aspects of ourselves are those things which you have chosen to manifest in abundance on your planet in terms of creating joy and abundance and sharing.

Ptaah: Very well stated.

Question: By that same token then, I guess those negative aspects of this planet are those things that you have chosen not to experience at all, things that we would think of in negative ways such as crime, etc.

Ptaah: We experience them to the extent that we observe you, and know that this is not for us. There was a time in our past when some of this experience was allowed. But it was, you might say, nipped in the bud by those who were wiser.

Question: You have stated previously: "But we have taken on certain tasks, such as for example the supervision of developing life in space, particularly human, and to ensure a certain amount of order." Is that in a sense seeding planets? Is that one way of interpreting that?

Ptaah: Seeding them in thought, you might say. There are a great many human and almost human races on planets. We will check up on them, so to speak, to see how they are doing, and will occasionally try to influence them in positive ways, if we feel they are ready, or if they are desirous of our inclusion in their way of life. But as far as seeding planets, as far as also colonizing planets, we do not choose at this time to colonize. Seeding is a term which really applies more to an entire creation of thought. Creating entire universe from thought to physical form, something we really do not do, do not have a total understanding of this, though perhaps slightly better than your own understanding. We have some considerable control over our physical environment, and some considerable understanding of our spiritual environment. But we are not at a point in time, in this physical reality which we live in, where we can literally create and re-create a reality to the point of being seeders of planets or seeders of universes.

Question: You've also said: "We feel duty bound to the citizens of Earth because our forebearers were their forebearers." Would that mean then that you and I share a common heritage in a sense?

Ptaah: Oh yes indeed. We do share this common heritage in our human beingness. Our forefathers were indeed your forefathers, though our civilization is somewhat older than yours, when you take into account our development. You might say that when Akashiel passed on, so to speak, into your past, we continued developing along those lines. We did not choose to experience negativity but continued.

So you see, while you experienced negativity, and went through various changes and upheavals, we kept on going, and that is why in positive social structures and entertaining enlightenments, we have gone on ahead of you. But not ahead in any way as far as being better, no. Only as far as learning more about ourselves, and being more in touch with ourselves.

Question: In terms of your planetary system, which we see as a cluster of stars, within that cluster is there what we think of as a single planet or central star, in terms of organization?

Ptaah: There is what you might call a central planet, a form of clearinghouse for information and social order. There is this planetary configuration within the star-system that you know as the Pleiades, and there are many planets within our influence that are situated around this star-system. 166 in number of planets, not all of them physical. 93 physical planets. More than one would expect. Some of them are not exactly moons but large asteroids which we choose to call planets.

Question: And there is travel amongst those planets?

Ptaah: Oh yes, absolutely. A sharing of commonality and social occasions, gatherings such as that.

Question: In terms of the universe, would your culture stand unique in the universe in what you have created, or are these other cultures existing along the same lines as yours?

Ptaah: Understand that we have not explored every single planet in the universe, but all individuals are unique also. I understand what you want to know here. We are not completely unique. There have been certain developments on Jupiter, certain facets especially having to do with underground cities. There are other planets which have developed along similar lines, and some which we have encouraged. So, no, we are not unique. There is no reason why you cannot develop also along these lines. We consider it our duty and our pleasure to encourage this type of growth if it is desired. We do not thrust it upon anyone, but are here to help if you should choose to come into our way of life, or any facet of our way of life.

Question: Are there any other planets who you choose to help, who are like us in terms of our progress?

Ptaah: Currently there are nine other projects on other planets going on simultaneously within the time-framework. There are these nine other projects in progress at this time, but none of these planets are within your immediate solar system.

Question: Would you, for instance, choose to spend most of your lifetime on a mission such as the one you're involved with, or is it something that is more brief in our terms?

Ptaah: We do not, as consciousness from Zeta Reticuli will, devote really a lifetime to a particular project. We do not do that. It is within our nature to need outlets, creative outlets, so our missions then will be for perhaps months in duration, then back to the planet for some healthful outlets, some forms of creativity, and sometimes even within one week of your time we will go back for a couple of days. Strictly to R & R, you might say in your terms. Rest and recuperation. Of course, there's no real recuperation needed but exploration of our artistic nature. Those expressive abilities which we have we must express, and with groups of our own kind, you understand, not really available here on this planet.

Question: You can go in your craft, to your planet and back?

Ptaah: Exactly. We can go directly to the planet in our craft.

Question: And it takes seven hours of our time?

Ptaah: Yes, you are correct. Seven hours of your time.

Question: Then would interplanetary travel be something that is done for pleasure?

Ptaah: Not totally for pleasure. it can be done for pleasure, that is encouraged, but it is mostly done to assist others, especially those whom we feel a kindred spirit with, such as Earth.

Question: Does everyone on your planet get to experience interplanetary travel on your craft, or are you revered as an astronaut, so to speak?

Ptaah: I am not revered in any way, only recognized as myself. I do not wish to lecture you on this point, but it is a point which needs to be cleared up. All individuals are encouraged to astral-project and recall totally their experiences. There is no need to experience interplanetary travel on craft exclusively. The need is to experience, as you say, interplanetary travel, singularly.

This way it is possible to absorb what you need to absorb and you can do this now. We do make missions on the craft in order to assist, bring equipment, and also to encourage those who would care to come aboard the craft and experience a small taste of our way of life as we show it to them at any given point in their time.

I will describe at the moment how I see the interior of our craft. We believe, in our system, in living art. We take it with us wherever we go. As I look about the interior of the craft, I see the color. The color is in the air. It has its own fragrance. It produces its own tone if you wish to hear it. The tones can be musical depending upon your state of mind. You simply reach up, touch the color as it floats about and feel the tones rhythmically vibrating through your body with their own musical clarity. Our art as we know it is living art, much as your art existed in Atlantis and in Lemuria.

We exist as extensions of those times and have continued certain social structures, one of them being a multi-sensual art consciousness.

The interior of the craft does have the usual navigational systems, but we do circulate this living, flowing color which appears as a gaseous cloud, flowing one color, mixing with another, but the original colors maintaining their own integrity. Colors viewed would be from your primary colors, but they have within them, you might say, floating flecks of small universes. If you could explore one of these small flecks, it would appear to have a very small universe, star system, thought structures, and all forms of diversity floating within a single fleck, which you might actually see as the metallic fragment disc floats within the color and reminds us of the diversity of all life. The craft exists interdimensionally.

Question: You mentioned once having a green sky. Is that a result of your atmosphere?

Ptaah: Yes it is. The atmosphere which is present there, but it is also of our choosing. We are comfortable with this light shade of green. It stimulates us, but basically we have this atmosphere, which is very similar to yours, primarily oxygen. We just choose to have this light green color because it is so pleasant and easy to live with, and we find it also somewhat spiritually uplifting.

Question: How about in terms of what we would call weather and seasons?

Ptaah: Well, we know we create our own reality. We can have weather in seasons if we wish it, but for the most part the weather we choose to have will be sunny. There will not be rain storms, snow and all that sort of thing, but we can create that environment if we wish to. It is not needed in order for things to grow comfortable and in order for there to be a constant abundance and necessary atmosphere.

Question: What about bodies of water? Do you have large bodies of water like our oceans?

Ptaah: Not as you understand them. We could have water to the extent of ice, but the ice is not cold to the touch since we do not believe in discomfort. It is strictly smooth and can be experienced as a texture and as a feeling.

Water can be experienced on many different levels, is usually done so in the underground cities, experienced running out of various water outlets. It can be experienced as a liquid. It can be rubbed between the hands and will feel somewhat like an oil, if we choose to perceive it that way. Water then, you might say, is a medium for self-expression.

Question: In terms of your plant life, what similarities might there be with our flowers, trees, fruit, vegetables and that sort of thing?

Ptaah: Well, the leaves on our trees are quite similar. Really, there is a great similarity, only there is greater variety of various forms of plant life which are now extinct on your planet and still present on our planet. There are more, as you say, succulents. We find them to be a most comfortable and reassuring sort of plant. It is hard to describe why, we just find them pleasant to be around. We do consume a fruit which is similar to your Australian Kiwi fruit. We have large melon-types of fruit which grow on trees. We try to grow our fruit and vegetables on trees, as it is more convenient, rather than having it on the ground.

Question: How about animals on your planet?

Ptaah: As we choose to experience them, we will create them, although they do have feelings and an identity of their own when they are created. We create them with care, since an animal which is created does not die per se, but goes on in that existence. For animals it is a land of no death. They experience their own existence and share their thoughts and their perceptions with us telepathically.

You know, you can learn to do this with your now animals on your now Earth. And will probably choose to preserve species and reincarnate species who have chosen to cease to exist now, in your new world as you create it.

Cats especially. Cats have more understanding of their abilities, and also sea creatures. Dolphins, turtles, whales, especially them.

Question: Do you have a time structure on your planet?

Ptaah: There is no need to experience time. Only a need to experience experience.

Question: Do you sleep and eat--those types of physical activity that we identify that way?

Ptaah: We sleep, not to the extent that you do here on Earth, because we find that it stifles creativity to sleep too long. What we generally do is sleep for two hours, and then perhaps later on within a period of time, which we do not call a day, but a twenty-hour period of time, we may wish to take a nap, a rest we call it, for perhaps another hour. We do not require the great quantity of sleep since our body structures are in a better form of balance, consistently, rather than just a temporary situation.

We eat a vegetarian, you might say, diet.

Question: Then your digestive system could be similar to ours?

Ptaah: Yes, only smaller. Without the need to absorb meat or anything heavy like that, it can be considerably smaller.

As you say being overweight--this is not something we are. We all tend to be fairly thin and there is no overweight but a balance--a physical balance as well as mental and emotional.

Question: Is it necessary for you to exercise? Do you need exercise to maintain your physical shell?

Ptaah: We maintain our fairly muscular--for men--looks without exercise as you understand it. Only by believing in beauty.

Question: What is your average lifespan in our terms?

Ptaah: One hundred and seventy-three years.

Question: Does your food require preparation? I mean, a

fruit for example, would you just eat it directly from the tree?

Ptaah: That is fairly close to what we do, yes. We can prepare something to make it look more beautiful, but generally we will eat raw fruits and vegetables, as the nutrients from them are more readily assimilated into our systems in a more positive way. We can create them, cut them up and make them look beautiful, but generally do not cook them as you understand. We do not use dairy products, though there is nothing wrong with them on your planet. We simply do not use them. We do not need them.

Question: Do you require water for the maintenance of your bodies?

Ptaah: We absorb a liquid which is not totally like your water, but is laced with all the basic nutrients which we need to sustain life as we understand it. This is our absorption of water.

Question: Is there anything associated with the communal aspect of sharing food, sharing a meal as we experience it?

Ptaah: You mean a large community meal together?

Question: Well, I guess emotionally, there is a certain significance to sharing food amongst ourselves--at least there used to be and, I feel, on certain levels it's coming back again.

Ptaah: This is encouraged at least one day of the week. But always you see, when we wish to eat, when we are ready to take in nourishment, anyone who is passing may join. There isn't a matter of personal outlay--I have to go down to the store and buy food--it isn't like that. The food is provided by the community. We all do our part and it is provided, and we encourage each other to be with each other. If someone is passing and is hungry, we invite them and we all join together and eat.

Question: Then there really is no such thing as a stranger on your planet...
Ptaah: No.
Question: ...everybody lives in communion, I guess, with one another?
Ptaah: There are no strangers on our planet. We are all of the same love. A harbinger of peace amongst us, a will to live together and create our own harmony. There are no outcasts on our planet. Individuals, yes. Families, yes. But community is something which is encouraged and stimulated from the time of birth.
Question: Is there any sort of what we would consider an economic system?
Ptaah: Well, you know, we feel that we can produce what we need. There is no economic system as you understand it, but there is a system of, shall we say, allowing that which we need to grow, and we live off of it. There is community sharing experience, as far as providing and distributing that which is needed to those who need it.
Question: In that context, is there what we would think of as a work situation? Not something that people don't want to do, but jobs that people choose to do?
Ptaah: Well, this is not a situation where I am talking about people loading trucks or something like that. We have certain abilities which we have utilized on the planet, some of them involving tones, some involving strictly mind thoughts--you might say telekinesis. We can move that which we need to move, those physical objects. We can move them without brute strength. We do not choose to fight the elements, but to work with them. So jobs per se do not involve difficulty, but only adjusting ourselves to that which needs to be done, and doing so in the most pleasant way possible, in the most spiritual, uplifting way; and occasionally in communion

with others through the use of tones.

This correlates to an experience on your planet which was taking place, a considerable amount of your time ago, in some occasions ancient Egyptians, in some occasions in South America. Some of these instruments are still in use. They look something like one of your folk instruments--a potato pipe, if you know what that is. They look like a very short flute. When these instruments are blown, it is possible to create the tones which will move physical objects.

We will sometimes still use these instruments as a form of community get-together. We do not actually need the instruments. We can make the tones ourselves or we can make internal, silent tones. But occasionally, when we wish to get together and have this community project to move some large object, we may wish to do so together. Perhaps we shall move a large object and cause it, not strictly to move from point A to point B, but maybe to jump around and dance around in the air to our satisfaction and joy. We also might wish to do that to entertain the children, showing them what they can do (Figure 1).

Question: What forms of transportation or mass transportation do you use?

Ptaah: Of course, as far as experiencing things, we will use astral projection. But as far as moving the physical body from planet to planet, we will use craft as you understand them. As far as getting around on the surface of the planet, we will use a certain amount of underground transit system. I would describe it in some cases like what you might call a tube system. But we also can move ourselves from one point on the planet to another point on the planet without using a machine. At this point in time I will not explain how we do that.

The tube system is essentially a machine which is left over from ages ago, but we still continue to use it since

Figure 1

PLEIADES— TELEKENESIS GAME

machines on our planet do not fall into disrepair but maintain themselves. We do not believe in creating disrepair. A machine is produced. It will last forever. We believe this and it is so. Remember, simplicity is the key.

Question: In terms of housing, do you have what we would consider a home of your own...

Ptaah: Yes (Figure 2).

Question: ...a certain place where you live or create?

Ptaah: Yes. You see, our population is somewhat controlled. We choose to control it to the point where we will not have a crowded situation, so there is no reason not to have a home of our own. We will tend to use more translucent and transparent materials, since our society is more open. Love is a natural thing, that is encouraged, and we do not hide what we do. Not to say that we don't have privacy if we choose it. We do have our own private homes, we just have a stronger feeling for community.

Our private space does not require a great deal of space as you will use. All we really will require is living space and resting space, and they will not be separate houses per se but large complexes, not fifty stories tall or anything, generally no more than three stories tall, and then not approached with stairs but more like ramps.

Question: Then you do live in communities. Do you have what we would call cities?

Ptaah: Yes, we do have cities, as you say, and we have as we call green areas, though not all the planet life is green, of course. There is this compatibility between the green on the ground and the green in the air. Our sky is green. There is this then compatibility and, you might say, recycled color.

So we do have cities then. Many of our cities are underground. Not because the surface of the ground is polluted, but strictly to make space, to allow more

Figure 2

PLEIADES— LIVING SPACE

surface green areas and more surface art cities. You might say crystal cities though they are not made of crystals, they are habited. But they will look somewhat like growing cluster of crystals from a distance (Figure 3).

Question: Could you discuss the "seashell buildings" I have heard about on your planet?

Ptaah: It is artistic development. All forms of art are encouraged. Seashell is not exactly what exists. A curvature, a flowing, but hollowed out on one side and spewing forth what seems to be a city. From one angle of approach, may appear to be a seashell. But to give you an idea, what this may look like in your terminology, allowing for certain differences, you might say a cornucopia. Do you understand what this is? As in a horn which large amounts of objects are coming out of. However, there is no horn coming back but strictly a curved area which looks to individuals who are not familiar with that very much like a large seashell.

Those who come to this planet find great beauty in your seashells as they exist and do produce certain non-physical duplications on the planet, and there are plans to produce several cities based upon these architectural elements. There are certain small buildings which are based upon the general shape of conch shells.

Question: Could we hope to see some of these things incorporated on this planet in our future?

Ptaah: You can do a great deal to encourage that with your writings. Stimulate the ideas which already exist. Allow people to feel as though they *can* do which they know they can do. You might say patting them on the back in words, and letting them know it's all right to do that which they would like to do.

It is an important task to put out this positive information. It is a most trustworthy situation, but

Figure 3

PLEIADES— SURFACE BUILDINGS

unfortunately there are a great many people on your planet who think of us as having horns and antennas. We shall, with each other's assistance, see what we can do to alter that unwarranted image.

Question: Would you care to go into ideas of social structure as they exist on your planet? In terms of family, and maybe friendship--do you form life-time links with another individual?

Ptaah: I will give you a brief overview. We do have a similar structure as on your planet, but with certain exceptions. We may wish to take a life-mate, a life companion, but there is no social pressure to do so whatsoever.

Beauty, you understand, physical beauty is something which we choose to express. So there is no aging as you understand it. An allowance toward the end of the life cycle for the body to simply change into a form which is comfortable. Just a change, a smooth transition from one physical shell into another, a, you might say, death experience from your point of view. But from our point of view, rather a smooth transition, you might say into reincarnation.

Now as far as social structures, as far as the family goes, to get back to that--you may wish, or one may wish, to take this life-mate and to have children. Same way as on this planet! And, you understand, this is an act of love. Love is positivity, therefore this is something which is worthwhile.

Children are raised within this family structure. Children can receive affection from all sources, as they grow to maturity. Experiencing various forms of community arts and crafts and developing their own singular forms of art expression, craft abilities, and the performing arts, which are necessary to function in a society such as ours. We are all performers to this extent.

Community theater is a form of community acting.

Acting not as you understand it, but rather a community experience.

Question: If two people choose to be life-mates or to form a union, is there a "marriage institution" involved? Would they choose to enter that sort of union as we think of it, or would it be just a more personal sort of commitment?

Ptaah: There is a commitment, very much as you have stated; a commitment which is just a word or bond between these two individuals, such as the two state to each other, "I choose you, to live with you, to be with me for all my tomorrows in this physical form," something like that. It will vary between individuals, but that is really the entirety of the ceremony per se, though if people wish to make a larger thing out of it, a party so to speak, that is encouraged also. Any facet of celebration and enjoyment and community-shared experience is always encouraged and occasionally people will wish to do this.

Question: How about education of the children? How does that take place or is it necessary?

Ptaah: Not as you understand it. It takes place in this theatrical culture. Children are encouraged to develop their own abilities. You might say to educate themselves through a form of constant self-creation, self-understanding.

This way, you see, they can come to understand why we choose to live our form of life.

Question: On your planet do children play games and do these games have a purpose in their development?

Ptaah: Our children will play games which will be geared toward, as you say, their development. Games which will organize their thoughts in joyful ways. They will be taught to move objects into patterns which are conducive to their development. They will be let into a room where

27

there will be many brightly colored bits and pieces. Then they will be shown a picture. It is almost like your jigsaw puzzle, but they will be informed they can't touch the pieces. They must form the picture without touching the pieces. They will receive a small illustration, but when these objects are put together it will be very large. The small illustration does not reveal too many details. So, of course, they are immediately curious about how to go about doing this. So they will begin to experiment. They will think about the pieces moving.

If it is necessary, they will be guided in techniques to utilize this method that you call telekinesis. They will, in time, form the pieces up. They will first experiment with one or two pieces. They all do this and the pieces will float about in the air and at first they will be attracted to the idea of being able to float objects about in the air, so this will keep them happy for quite a while. In certain amount of time they will then begin to form the pieces together. Now they are not notched like your puzzle, they are just bits and pieces, you might say like tile only not really this solid--more of a flexible material. They will then form these pictures in air utilizing these bits and pieces.

Now they will have to concentrate enough to be able to keep the pieces in the air. They will truly have to focus all of their energies into the act of keeping more than one piece balanced. It is like juggling, only without the use of your hands. So there might be at any moment a thousand or fifteen hundred or more pieces hanging in the air, so to speak. They will form this picture, whatever picture we choose, as in time as they get better at this, then they can move the colors about, you see, move them about and form any picture they want.

This is really a beginning toward the idea of forming colors out of the air, but first they start at a young age.

Step by step. It is a game which is designed to teach a skill, which is designed to be experienced with joy. So they will use these bits and pieces of colored chips, so to speak, and create a picture and in time create their own pictures, and in time, if they choose, can create sculptures out of light.

The idea with these games obviously is to encourage skills which can be useful not only on our planet but elsewhere, if they are needed as consultants when they become adults. They can form necessary objects out of thin air, so to speak.

Question: In terms of what we would consider an education for the children, is there a formal structure of any sort in your system--teaching the children social skills and what we would consider intellectual development?

Ptaah: Not in the form of a rigid disciplinary structure. It is set up more on the basis of individuals who will choose to have children will then literally take the responsibility for the education of their children into their own hands. They will participate as, in this case, mother, father, teacher and, as all teachers know when they participate with students, they are also students. They will then have for themselves as parents a learning experience while teaching. All teachers know to do this, and hence on your planet will do this at times. It is a form of responsibility for the entire over-seeing of the young ones' lives.

When the proper age is reached, then the young ones may choose to go out and about to receive education from other sources, but until the children reach the age of what you would perceive as about fifteen years old, parents are still in charge of their education, though they can go about to other parents, you might say. Any child is welcome in any home on Pleiadian-influenced planets. Children are considered treasures, joys, as they are in many circumstances on your planet but not all.

So they are always welcomed into every home, and every individual, whether they are actually performing the parental role or not, can, if they choose, be a teacher or a student depending on the moment.

Question: What kind of toys might the children use, and again, would the toys play a role in their education and development?

Ptaah: They will always be encouraged to form their own toys once they have learned the picture-puzzle game. The whole thrust of this game is to encourage them to be able to utilize Liquid Light. It is really a form of technology, but it is also connected to thoughts in the sense that without thoughts and clear emotions, Liquid Light technology will not function, except at the level of what you might call autonomic, at a level that is not influenced by the conscious mind.

Question: Our children are taught very young to order and classify the environment through the use of play materials and such. It sounds like it might be fair to say that your children are taught to do the same thing, only our ordering is more physical where yours would be more mental.

Ptaah: I would not refer to what we do with our children as to create order, but in the sense that you mean it, as far as being able to focus energy or intensity on any one subject at any one moment, yes, it is a way of, you might say, creating order within the thought processes, or fine-tuning the thought processes. It is through this method that the arts are created, in the sense of mobile physical sculptures. So that artisans can be involved in their work by use of fine-tuning Liquid Light; and yet in order to do this, they must be able to order their minds, order their spirits, order their emotions, order their focus to within a range that they must concentrate fully on what they are doing.

Yet they are not ordering themselves out of a form of discipline. It is more out of the joy of knowing what is to come of their art. They are not isolated from the rest of society, they can see all around them what others have done, and it gives them some idea of what they might do in technique. Not necessarily specifically what they must do as far as copying, because your mind will always be creative, just as your consciousness will always be creative.

So anything which is thought can be created in Liquid Light technology (Figure 4). This is why we do not choose to experience negativity. Because, just consider, if you were able to create anything out of Liquid Light, consider how necessary it would be to be involved in positive creative efforts.

You could say that what you do on your planet is an effort to incorporate negativity in a way in which it would be useful to your experience. However, we do not choose to involve ourselves in that form of experience.

Question: So in that framework then, there is no need created for what we would consider discipline in regard to children?

Ptaah: Exactly. Just the opposite. The children see all around them what can be done with this ability to focus their concentration at any one point at any one moment. They see what can be done and they desire to be a part of it.

It is always encouraged in a joyful manner. Happy manner. Which is why I like to joke around with you, my friend. It is something which, on your planet, it would be a good idea to have a little more of: Joy.

Question: What do you do if immature desires sometimes have not particularly desirable results?

Ptaah: Only if one chooses to experience negativity would undesirable events take place, but if you take

Figure 4

PLEIADES— LIQUID LIGHT INSTRUCTION

negativity out of the perception, emotions, thoughts, what would be undesirable?

Question: What type of art might be seen in your homes?

Ptaah: This would be similar sculptures, created by the participants, in order that the art would be fully compatible. It is that the art in these mass events, you might say, are fully compatible, but in the home structure, in the home environment, individuals who have been trained in this artisan capacity, and most people on the Pleiades have some familarity with this background since they were all children at one time.

They will create a smaller version of this form of sculpture. Where you will have in your living rooms a radio, stereophonic music, they will have instead this form of sculpture. When individuals wish to experience tones which are pleasing to them, they can either touch the sculpture. They will hear in the form of vibration through the body.

Or, if they choose not to touch the sculpture, they can telepathically place within the sculpture the harmonious tones of the immediate family group. For any passers-by or friends who are there, the sculpture will then balance the tones and create those pleasing sounds which will help to raise their joy consciousness, which is always present and yet at times like that will reach a form of ecstasy.

Question: What forms other than Liquid Light sculpture would the visual arts take on your system?

Ptaah: There will be, when music is created, perhaps created out of a mass gathering of people and will create tones, either telepathic tones, vibrations, or will create actual out-loud, as you understand it, tones. If they choose, these tones can form colors. If you can visualize, imagine an individual making a tone which is the right tone for them and calming. Their own special tone, as you all have. Imagine a stream of color coming out of their bodies, floating up above them and intertwining with all the other individuals' colors. Not only does that create beautiful patterns of flowing and ebbing color, but it is felt on a vibrational level by all the participants (Figure 5). Thus art is created from tone.

Question: Do you have musical instruments as we think of them? Do you form musical groups, as we would think of bands, orchestras or choirs--that sort of thing?

Ptaah: Yes, we do have instruments to some extent. We also do a sort of harmonious toning. I can describe an instrument to you which would be, on your instrumental scale, a form of reed instrument. It looks somewhat like a flute, only it is curved. It has holes, and is held in this sort of a manner. You see, it is quite comfortable to hold an instrument that curves around like this. In this way you can rest your arms. It does not weigh anything. It is not heavy. It is essentially an instrument which utilizes tones in the format of a flute, and there are other instruments along this idea.

Generally, our instruments will use light, airy tones pleasant on the ears, not brass such as you. Not that there is anything wrong with brass, but we just choose not to create those sounds. We would prefer sounds which are somewhat natural, so to speak, like wind songs, wind sounds you see; wind sounds which create wind songs. A flute is an instrument very compatible with this.

We also have an instrument which looks something like a flute, only it curves around in other fashions and is sort of an extension. It is an interesting instrument in that two people play it. Again, there is this kind of grasp, and another person on the other side. There is a person here, holding the instrument as it goes into the

Figure 5

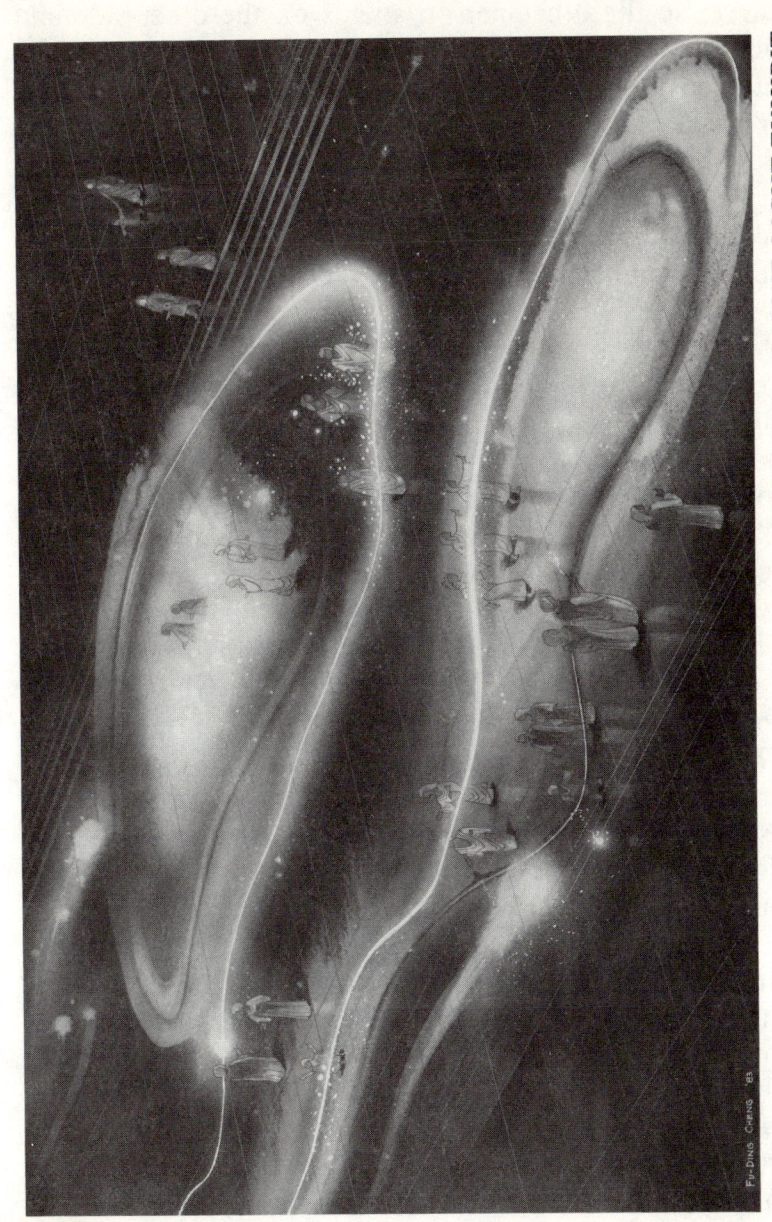

PLEIADES— LIQUID LIGHT EXHIBIT

mouth. It curves around this way also, like an "S" curve, so the other person stands on the other side and plays holding the arms the same way, so there is this sort of facing each other feeling. So the musicians not only create a harmony in a tonal structure, but also create a harmony in being able to see each other (Figure 6).

Being involved directly on the same instrument, and seeing each other playing the instrument, and feeling this certain ambient pleasantry feeling from both the musicians is most comfortable and compatible to us.

As far as choral groups, or singing groups, yes, people are encouraged in a way. Not the same format, but in a similar fashion as your barbershop quartet. Groups of people--four or five, six or seven individuals--might wish to get together and sing songs which appeal to them. This is an important factor. They are comfortable with songs or music which they might make up. It feels comfortable within their entire systems, and they sing it.
The people who listen then, who stop to listen in any area within the city, are those people who also feel comfortable with those tones and those sounds. Therefore you have compatibility, not only within the group who is singing, but with the group who is listening. Everyone who is participating then is experiencing a pleasant, comfortable feeling within their minds and souls as they absorb these wonderful sounds.

There are also situations where people will sing in a singular fashion, only stopping to sing and sharing their life experience to some extent by singing songs that you might say come from the heart about their experience, or about that which they will experience or that which they might choose to experience or even that which has been experienced by others who are close to them. These might be referred to, from your point of view, as folk songs.

There is not a commercial music distribution like you

Figure 6

PLEIADES— "S" SHAPED FLUTE

have here, radio stations, such as that. We find that sort of thing will tend to separate individuals from the music. We would prefer to have contact music, so to speak, almost like a contact sport. Persons singing, people playing instruments, actual contact, the audience being there present hearing it. There is not a situation where you might miss something.

Nothing is missed because there is a form of recording in that the air . . . this is complicated, but the air sort of has its own memory. The people who would like to experience that which has been shared in some area musically, and as the gathering has left, can come by later on and touch certain points within the area and hear everything, feeling it also. The points that they touch are what you might say keys. They're like panels with colors. They can put their hands or just a finger, or just one hand, or any part of their body which they would like to on the panels. The panel also changes color, if they wish. It will show the multitude or the small group who was there before, experiencing the music, and they can, if they choose, experience the group's experience, so that they would feel as though they were a part by experiencing it.

So there is this structure, a continuing structure, of the audience experience. The experience of one who is not actually producing the sounds, but the simpatico feelings with the instruments, and the tones and the musicians, by experiencing them from the listeners' point of view.

I am trying to provide you with a glimpse at our social structure through our artistic consciousness, since you are sensitive to this type of what you might perceive as futuristic art or multi-imaging art. On our planetary system, we utilize a great deal of play within our social structures, since play is a universal relaxant for all individuals of our physical type. Physically we are almost identical to you, though we have made some inroads as far as controlling negative emotions. You will really have to do this also if you wish to advance to the point of being able to travel through dimensions, since thought-form is a method that you will probably utilize. Negative thoughts or emotions taking place during a thought-form transition can cause the craft and all occupants to, you might say, detour into what could become negative space, to the extent of a possible unpleasant experience. So a centering of positive thought during this time of re-imaging from one physical world to another is critical.

Interplanetary connections such as your planet is only now beginning to recognize will result in the assistance of your accelerating effort towards your new age. You will find us, as with many others from other worlds, to be willing teachers and happy, you might say, since we are also eager to experience your feelings.

As far as bringing our arts with us on the craft to your planet, and providing our arts to you, as far as making them available in thought, I shall say that holographic sculpture is really beyond your singular capacities at this time, as you understand it, though of course you can do it. You are not ready to express that side of yourself. But as far as music, we try to experience music within a story, you might say. Tones permeating our bodies and our immediate space within the craft. Tones which we find compatible with our physical selves--we are physical. These tones then will frequently be those tones that are most comfortable within our physical bodies, and this is something you can do. You can experiment by making your own tones, humming or singing, finding that octave range which is most comfortable for you, and thence listening to music, or even recording music by singing or playing an instrument and staying within that octave range of tones which are most compatible for your physical self. You may find this type of music most soothing, and it might just bring out certain hidden talents within you. There are certain latent abilities, we shall say, which are present within all physicals on Earth. Exploring your own tonal range, we can call this. This is certainly an exercise which any physical can do, and is a possibility for all individuals, in all places, at all times.

Music, then, for us is this self expression. We will sometimes organize our previous experiences into a melody and sometimes organize the experiences, as we perceive them, of other individuals within a tune which is comfortable with them. We can, by use of a tool which is somewhat similar to your mass spectrometer, tune into frequencies which all physical beings have in common, though there will be from individual to individual slight variance within tonal structures, within the comfort zone. We can use this tool on individuals to find their comfort octave zone, if you understand.

The tool in no way comes in touch, physical touch, with any physical being, but is essentially what you might call a sensing device, utilizing high-frequency sound waves to, you might say, feel out your sensitivity.

The music we play then is environmental stimulus to our own creative thoughts. This is precisely what can be done by you in finding your own octave range. You might find that playing this octave range, which is comfortable for you, will stimulate your creativity. But even if it does not, it will certainly make you feel comfortable and at peace with yourself.

Question: By this octave range do you mean, for instance, certain chords like, say, on a piano? I know there are certain chords that I feel comfortable with. Now when I play the piano, I move outside of an octave range--meaning eight notes. Do you mean staying within that eight-note octave range?

Ptaah: Not necessarily. There are overlapping, shall we say, notes within a chord. What you can do is play chords in such a way that there is basic tonal symphonic similarities. Find those tones even if a chord should be outside of any particular octave. Find the tones which are most sympatical with you, you know, compatible and stimulating. You must search out your own range. A single octave range may not be for you. By octave range I do not mean one octave. It could be infinity as far as your ability to hear sounds physically, though do not discount your ability to absorb the sounds in an ultrasonic fashion. This is when tones come into the picture.

A single octave, then, is not the way it must be, but only an example for your reference.

Question: The tool that is similar to a mass spectrometer, is that for use on your planet, or is it something you use here?

Ptaah: It is something which as been developed on our planet and is an instrument which is on the craft, all craft, which is used to make contact with individuals on your planet, and on all craft with ability to travel from this dimension to our home planet. Sometimes they are not on what we would call shuttle craft, since those craft are not usually used to contact individuals. That is the placement of this instrument, this machine. It is not used to any great extent on our planet, for there are other methods on our planet for tuning into our own populus.

Question: What influence might you have in what we consider our artistic community, as awareness of your reality unfolds on our planet?

Ptaah: It is hoped that artisans in your community will begin to use holographic spectrum art. They will perhaps get together with technicians and form, really, technical artisans. It would be very much like a new job, where it would be necessary for people involved with computer graphics and other individuals involved with technological forms to create holographic images.

Music can then be provided by your current abilities, perhaps live music such as musicians standing nearby playing a flute or some such pleasant instrument, and people could walk around and through these sculptures and get somewhat of an idea what is possible. There would not be sculptures in your sense, but would truly be computer graphics. Lights floating in the air which could be regulated by technical artisans working from a computer base.

Question: So our current progress in computer graphics is a stepping stone toward this?

Ptaah: Yes.

Question: Would this tie in to what we consider to be video entertainment?

Ptaah: Yes, very good! It has the potential in time for creating a home entertainment system where individuals can utilize their computers. In time, computers will not have keyboards as you recognize them, but will have contacts which will connect to the fingers, and there will be a sensing system involved. But these forms can be created then in thin air by the individual who then would truly feel a part of his own art. He will be his art, and his art will be a representation of him, as he will be creating colors and patterns holographically in his own home. It is a good stepping stone toward understanding that art is truly created by the artist and truly appreciated by those who are involved in its creation.

Question: I'm starting to get a little bit of an understanding of Liquid Light. I want to understand how that is used visually. I'm sure children as well as adults are able to use it in any way they choose. Is this Liquid Light technique a way of creating a form of matter in whatever thought patterns you desire at a given time?

Ptaah: Exactly.

Question: Is there any way we could train ourselves here to utilize this technique?

Ptaah: Right now it would be better for you to concentrate on eliminating the need for negativity within your emotional framework, because if you learned that technique right now you would only, casually, bring forth unnecessary negative acts. You do not have, right now, the way, the willingness to focus intensely on any one moment and maintain positive emotions. Purity of thought. You will, in the future of your time. Right now, it is all right to understand, but not a good idea to practice.

Question: Is this ability to focus clearly, to create these images, a biological function?

Ptaah: Not really. It is more a function of emotions. So if one chooses not to experience negativity in your range of emotions, you would find that it would not be necessary to create negative thought light spectrums.

Question: How is Liquid Light used on your planet? Is it used in your homes, your cities?

Ptaah: It is generally speaking done as what you might call now a mass event. There will be large groups of people nearby and an artist will choose to create a floating sculpture, one which involves color. This has been discussed somewhat before, but I will touch on it again as a large group of people would experience it.

It is a possibility, you know, that a floating sculpture can be created in the air, many different patterns floating about, and when an individual reaches up to touch that sculpture, they will be affected. They will hear the tones of that sculpture and bring them back to them. They will also, in their own right, affect that sculpture in color and tonal vibration. All other individuals who are present in that area would hear that vibration, would see the colors, and would choose on their own to be a part of it.

Now perhaps you would get more than one individual. You could get a very large sculpture, hundreds and hundreds of your feet long, floating in the air. Individuals could reach up, touch the sculpture. They would create a musical variety of tones, which would create, as you would see it, a song. Which would be, you might wish to say, a song of creative artistry. Truly melding art and music. You will have a representation of this on your planet when your artists will form a sculpture and play music in the background. They will know at an unconscious level that this other form of art exists, but have yet to express it. Though they will, in the future of your time, as they come into the abilities to be able to perform this technique and develop their own purity of thought and are able to focus their thoughts on the moment.

Question: Do these light sculptures take any form that we would recognize, such as animals, birds, trees?

Ptaah: Only if it is desired by the artist. The artist will set up the initial shape, but the participants can shape the sculpture into anything they wish, provided they are all of a like mind.

Question: Is the color involved in your Liquid Light art something that you not only see but also feel?

Ptaah: Yes. You are stimulated by certain colors, as they will stimulate emotions and have certain effects on you, remind you of certain abilities that you can perform. So it is, which will be generated by touch with the sculpture, will reveal abilities that all individuals have. The full color spectrum will realize the idea amongst the participants that they are capable of performing and creating any art which is necessary and beautiful for them to experience, art for others to experience. It is a way of reminding themselves that they are whole and complete as they exist.

On your planet you will use colors more and more in the coming years to remind you of your own abilities. Some of your individuals who will be involved in, as you see, spiritual techniques, will choose to wear forms of purple. Others will choose to wear very light colors. It is really a way you will use to activate your own possibilities and probabilities.

ORION

Orion the Hunter is a constellation visible from the Northern Hemisphere, lying on the celestial equator between Canis Major and Taurus. It contains the bright stars Betelgeuse and Rigel.

The Orion System is a large one, with many diverse planets within it. Orion is known throughout the universe for its intellectual development and for its music.

The source of this material is Zagat, who comes from the planet Troom. Troom is one of the many planets within what we call Orion.

Samuel has provided an introduction to the Orion material.

Orion is a very large place, you might say. Most life is humanoid in Orion, most life as you understand it. The planet Troom is but one planet in the system. We could spend 36.5 years discussing the others.

Orion is known for light, love and music. Light is intellect, with equal shares of spiritual growth and incorporation. It is what they are known for.

Light in this case meaning the light of insightful, all-knowing knowledge. Light itself is energy. Energy is all throughout the mass spectrum. Being, appreciated by the heart and mind.

Love is cherished and nurtured throughout all ages, past, present, future. Music representing the songs of the heart through all internal and external tones which can accompany language.

--Samuel

Orion is an idea, as is all existence. The source planet called Orion is the physical form. This planet's cultures have created down through the system you now know as the Orion galaxy.

My planet within the galaxy seeks to assist planets which are transitioning, such as yours. Our system of government is ruled by consensus.

The length of life is roughly 400 of your years. Discussions of politics are not relevant since consensus rule is absolute.

The planet itself is warm and dry. The soil is yellow, with brownish patches. The atmosphere is similar to yours, and you would be able to survive on the surface of the planet. The atmosphere is thin by your standards, and the planet is protected electronically from falling debris.

Work is divided equally among all members, according to their preference. The planet is not vegetated in your way--as you understand vegetation. It is more similar to the now surface of Mars, but less rocky. More of a desert-type surface.

Vegetation is encouraged within the cities for ornamental purposes only. Animals do not exist as you understand them, but are in large, open, zoo-type areas, where they are encouraged to live in harmony by creating friendly habitats for them. We do not have animals living with us, as you do.

Cities exist under clear, dome-like structures, a glass type of substance, but grown, such as crystals.

Our interest in your planet is not for reasons of looking after our own, or being involved with individuals like us. You would classify us as humanoid though; we look very much like you except for skulls, which are somewhat larger in circumference near the top of the head. A difference in radius.

We assist the network on your planet through the usual methods, and now--recently only--have become in contact with selected individuals. Other cultures have been contacting your culture for many years, but for us this is relatively recent--within the last 3.5 to 5 of your years.

We are now involved in contacting members--as you would say "direct aliens"--of our heritage. Those who are a little tardy are getting special attention and encouragement.

We are mostly involved then in planetary communication systems--between us and you, through contact individually and in small, very small, groups.

We are 38.5 light years from Earth. Depending on the route, it can also be 48.3. It takes us 6.5 hours of your time to make the trip.

Our current mission is 2.5 years of your time, but we will not always be around your planet. We will generally split the time between here and our native planet. The name of our planet is Troom.

We are usually about 6.5 feet tall, though there are those of us who are about 7 feet.

We have shown our craft publicly recently. Others from our planet and our system have also done so. Our craft will usually appear green in color, though there is no exclusion--we may wish to cause it to appear differently. There are other planets within the Orion constellation who have had long-term expeditions here. For us it is recent.

--Zagat

SATURN

The following material represents several contacts with a representative from a civilization on the planet Saturn, the sixth planet of our own star system.

From our current perspective, the Saturnian civilization exists in a different dimension of space-time than our own, in what we now would call our future. In sending craft to observe Earth in our time, they utilize a form of time-traveling which is at the heart of interstellar travel.

The contacts with the being from Saturn were among the first, and the representative has responded on several occasions to the question, "Why are you here?"

References to "Jupiterian Logic" relate to a system of thought or philosophy which originated on Jupiter but has now spread to other parts of the universe, where it is used with appreciation.

To help create a better mankind in the world of the future. The joy of the world to be built will be appreciated by those who live in it, walking upon the soil. Living amongst the living, not among dead hopes or beliefs. Creating a world that works, not one of wishes and dreams. That which has been created out of a need-- not created by simple wants or desires. Needs come first in the line of that which is served. If the world is to be created properly, then it must be created out of conscious need; therefore it is important to <u>be aware of the needs you are creating</u>. This is what is involved in purity of thought.

Thought purification is not something one goes to the laundromat for, but rather is when one is aware of one's thoughts. You might say, plugging into your own memory banks; thoughts of awareness, thoughts of calculation, thoughts of emotional vitality. The world will be better off for the more pure in thought, and that is the world that will be created out of necessity. Living in the world of the pure in thought will create the necessary contacts, contacts of the type which will allow you to grow and allow others to grow, if they choose.

We serve and take care of those who are willing to learn. Our mission is designed as strictly a peaceful one, but this has not always been so. It has on some occasions been involved in the most devastating of wars. But those days are behind us now.

Our craft will be seen in your skies from time to time, and will be noticed much more frequently.

Our world has nothing but love and encouragement for your world.

We chose to contact you through this method, since it is the most direct and is a way to funnel our information directly to you, if you are willing to learn it. We seek contact with you if you wish it only, not if you do not.

Our source, our planetary source, goes before you with all wisdom and encouragement. Our home is Saturn, the Saturn of the future in your terms of time. But it is in our current lives that we take, what you might say, a time journey and evolve our way to your present time in order to assist in the re-creation of your future. We do not intend in any way to interfere.

The method of transport for our craft is through crystal technology. The form of passage through time is not something I wish to discuss, but will say generally that it does cover thought-forms in what you might call lightening speed, necessitated by the passage and change of time to time--our time to your time, if you understand. Physical breakdowns of matter do not occur within this type of time-space, since there is a necessary thought formation which occurs before, during and after the actual flight. But actually it is more of a re-imaging technique from our time galaxy. Galaxy in this sense referring to a method of classification, time classification.

We are here for the purpose of intriguing your planet. Allowing creative energies to flow down and through the planet and invest the inhabitants with a sense of peace and willingness to learn and understand. It is our intention to stay within the area to promote harmony and justice.

Insight into understandings of human nature as they apply to <u>Jupiterian</u> nature. Our culture survives from the future and derives from your past. Our understanding of the nature of your events is brought about by your understanding of the nature of non-events. The establishment of our Flight Camp within your Southern California region was brought about by a desire to be close to this center of this New Age phenomenon, as it is perceived by the inhabitants of this area. Working within your structures, we try to bring about mutual and harmonic changes through the challenge of consistent interaction with members of your species, and projecting members of ours. We try to associate in any way which is useful and any type of functional situation is one in which we will have some sort of input. Not necessarily control, but a way of funneling or channeling the energy to reach its maximum possible solution.

Synchronicity of timing is vital within the nature of the flow of events. Finalizing the appropriate comments, really, a gesture of unity aboard the craft. All individuals aboard the craft will channel their thoughts to me so that I may channel my thoughts and their thoughts to you and others like you who are willing to receive. With this type of contact we believe initial solidarity can take place through the functioning of friendship partnerships. The desire for the long run, would be a union of souls, or an understanding of commonality. Features of our relationship would be the flashing of information from points of the universe to moments of your consciousness waking and on occasion in your dream state, for whatever may be the proper moment idea-point institutional crisis-solving solution.

We do not take in liquids in your fashion, but we tend to apply them to the surface of our bodies, more along the function of your bath but not actually a bath. A method of incorporating moisture without the use of a mouth, which we have really evolved, if that is the correct term, evolved out of our system, our physical system.

We look forward to future contacts should you wish them.

We are here to study your planet and its environment.

Human beings upon it, of course, but also the plants, animals, the fish, all creatures that walk, swim or crawl upon the face of your Earth. We, of course, are in our craft as always, in the immediate area.

The physical structure of our bodies externally is almost exactly that of your bodies. The only real difference is that with our breathing apparatus. We obtain some of our oxygen through what amounts to, well, it can be best described of as a system of gills, though they are not at all obvious to the casual observer.

Our purpose here is to study the evolution of your planet, and all species upon the planet, to bring you more in harmony with the universe, as you know it in your immediate area. We do not come from a great distance, such as others who are in nearby craft, but are more closely aligned with your solar system. Saturn is our home. Though it cannot be immediately seen from your space probes, since our colony is within the planet rather than without. We wish to bring about change to induce harmony into your world, or should I say to re-introduce harmony, since harmony does exist at many of your non-physical and even some of your physical levels--in the animal kingdom as you call it, and, of course, with plants and trees.

I would suggest that you observe the plants and trees to see how they come about with this harmony. A good study can be made and applied in a functional method, or a structural analysis method, and possibly may be useful in the transformation of your more violent ways, which are fortunately somewhat on the wane.

We feel that your planet in its entirety will alter its own course and come about to a more harmonious existence in your future of your time.

I might mention that time exists for us in a similar, but not exactly the same, dimension. It is so similar, however, that the difference is not that great. To give you an example, one of our days, if computed in your hours, would be approximately 24 hours and 57 minutes. Therefore you can see that there is not a great difference in our time structure, but a difference fairly miniscule.

We find your planet and you human beings upon it a most fascinating and worthy study for social scientists such as we. We do have other scientists on nearby craft from our planet, but they do not tend to intermingle with us. The scientific community is well bracketed, you might say. The social scientists mingle with each other on missions, and the more physical scientists mingle with each other also. The purpose of this is to try to avoid influencing the outcome of experiments while on missions here at your planet. There is no division, of course, when we are at home in our own group. The results, therefore, from our studies, it's hoped, will be more pure and consistent with the nature of the sub-group. We do compare notes with each other and we are in contact, but the specific studies going on on any of the craft are not discussed.

There are a great many craft around your planet. They are to be found with considerable concentration in the entire western half of your United States, but especially in desert regions and in some mountain regions, generally tending to seek out the more isolated areas. There are occasional forays into other areas, but infrequent outings over highly populated areas.

We have been encouraged to contact your species through the use of this form of ancient telegraph--the medium system--since it is believed that now is a good time to make our presence known, at least to small numbers, with the hope that the word will get out. We are here for good, and not for the purpose of containing or surpressing your population.

We will try to make available some knowledge we have

on the structures, and compatible and some incompatible groups within your structures, in order to bring about harmony.

I will describe our craft for you, so you may be able to pick it out, you might say, amongst the myriad of others that are here. I am sitting in front of a panel which you might consider a control panel. It slopes up away from me, my hands are on the panel in pre-marked areas. I function by channeling my thoughts out through my hands into the panel. The panel functions to amplify my thoughts and feed them back to me, clarifying the ones I wish to send. You can see the panel in your mind's eye and can, for that matter, see me from the back. My natural colored hair is a sort of orange color, cut closely. You can see my hands on the smooth, lit panel. There is another panel coming up vertically in front of me, also a smooth, well-lit panel, which is at this time clear of any instrumentality. However, instruments can be thought up on the panel by moving hands over areas which, by your understanding, would be switches, but there is no touching involved, just a motion of the hands over the area can call up certain instrument reviews or navigational information--you might say--computer banks.

We encourage your on-going progress as we are situated in our environment.

I will describe the immediate area to you. I am standing in front of a long, well-lit panel. The base is dark and supports a shelf with a back panel coming up, and is flat on top. A long, circular type of panel upon which various readings can be punched up, to use your terminology, though we do not have switches as you understand them but use a thought-command method.

We service many craft here. Supplies and information are passed back and forth here in a social intercommunication climate of mutual understanding and union.

Our function is that of a scientific outpost. We receive and channel information to our own craft from our mother planet and cooperate in the service to other craft from their planets. Recently we have begun channeling information directly to mediums on your planet to encourage your communion with our outpost here, on this level of communication, to try to draw you into the planetary community of understanding and social and scientific research.

We try to encourage this sort of a contact to help bring about the peaceful evolutionary forces of your planet and to let you know that there are others here from your lineage who support you and encourage you on your way and others of your immediate group to pass along information in any means which you can employ to encourage the peaceful progress of your planet towards a more union type of a goal. Union in this case meaning a utilitarian utopia.

We do not expect your planet to arrive at a situation like that in the immediate future, of course, but if one has a goal, well, we need only work towards it as long as we know what our goal is, is that not so? So we just want you to be aware of our presence. There are many presences from other planets in the immediate area. There are those amongst them who are representatives, who are willing to contact you and speak through you to pass along information which may be of some assistance.

ZETA RETICULI

Zeta Reticuli is a star system, or network of stars, visible only from the Southern hemisphere of our planet.

It is known for its technological development.

Joopah is the name of the representative from this system.

We would like to have you on the craft someday soon, if you wish it. Our mission is strictly one of peace and good will. Many are assisting in your planet's turnaround from negative to more positive paths for your future. Progress toward these eventual realities and goals will be allowed--will be allowed by members of your planet and mass.

We are here to assist you now in any way possible. For now, this method is suitable for you and your friends and associates. Try to visit us in such a manner (mediumship) more often, if you feel up to it.

You know our craft by the red light we will sometimes flash to you within your desert skies. Our planet and system, known as Zeta Reticuli, welcomes you and your friends in your attempt to make contact. You will be associated in contact, if you wish it, with various craft from various planetary systems.

I will reiterate, as others have, purity of thought--a discipline worthy of working on, my friend, a discipline worthy of all the individuals on your planet in order to bring about a more cohesive and positive regenerating community.

A timelessness can be created in positive environments, a world that will work in good ways. We can all create worlds that work. It is the desire for all peaceful peoples to create worlds that work peacefully, happily and joyously. For where is the desire by all men to become this happy, peaceful and stimulating group of individuals but in your hearts, in your minds, and in the very living tissues of your bodies. This is the life of the world to come. The world to come is the world which you are creating, and this is the life of your future. You will all live to see it, my friend. You will live to see it within the soul of your greater souls, within the heart of your greater hearts, and, if you choose, within the body of your greater bodies, through the eyes of the living tissues.

Seek that which is the finest, and expel that which has no value. For the world which you create will be one in which your children will live in joy and harmony. Finding that soul, power and light within us all is the worthiest task that can be asked of any man. Be of good cheer, my friends, for you will find upon wakening one day a world of great light and joy, and will know that you, in some way, have had a part in the creation of all this wonder.

You can do it by your own thought and belief. You can do it by your actions. You can do it in many ways and you will find them as needed. We will assist you in any way that we can. Seek us if you will. The finding will be joy to all, for the seeking is part of the educational learning process and will only be part of the greater joy upon the finding of the great treasure of friendship at the end of the path. Memories of our future fill my heart now, and I send you great love from your future time as I reside in your current space. Great success, my friends, from your friends of Zeta Reticuli.

The following message from Joopah opens by describing the interior of the craft from which the communication is originating, and goes on to talk about their movements around and near our planet.

A center console rises up out of what you could call the floor. There is a dark base. As you look at the base, it is dark. The next level up is a bright lighted area followed by a slightly darker area, followed at the top by a bulbous area which is used in the navigational system. This is also brightly lit. I will be sitting at this point, not staring into the navigational system but sitting nearby it in a utility type of seating device. The other members of the crew will not be within my sight, but will be off in other corners of the ship, in their quarters or doing what is possibly necessary in the maintenance of the craft. If they have any ideas or thoughts they wish to transmit to you, they will be thinking to me and I will pass these thoughts on to you.

The walls of the craft directly in front of me and to the sides of me incorporating my peripheral vision are dark except for a thin band of light at approximately ten of your inches above my eye level as I am sitting down. The thin band of light continues around the entire inner shell of the ship, or craft as you wish to call it. Behind me and out of my line of sight is a lighted area which you may refer to, if you see it, as a model area. There is a physical model of our universe which is lit from within, a clear structure behind which is a viewing screen upon which any navigational information or future travel areas can be viewed (Figure 7). An overlay of our universe is convenient to us and this is the reason for the model.

Our ship comes from the solar system which is be-beyond your system in light years.

We believe our area of the universe to be largely inhabited by members of the Zeta Reticuli group. This group influences many planets within the area, but does not dominate then in the sense that you may dominate or colonize a nation, but rather guides and directs the population to lead a more harmonious and productive

Figure 7

ZETA RETICULAE— INSIDE SPACE CRAFT

existence. Our ship does contain individuals of direct lineage from the Zeta Reticuli group. However, there are others on the ship who are not from this descendance. I myself am not directly from this descendance, but rather from the descendants of the *Faughn* group. This group is one which has not really been explored greatly in your society.

The ship is based within the Zeta Reticuli System and is a long-reach science function oriented group. We, for our part, do not wear uniforms as you understand them, but our clothing is of a simple nature which would appear to be a uniform to you. But is actually just this simple form of dressing which takes on the look of a uniform. It is black with gold flecks from the middle of the body down to the point where the legs attach to the body. Our height is approximately four and one-half of your feet. We have large, wide-spaced and long eyes. We do appear, all of us, to be descendants of the Zeta Reticuli formation of culture, though there are some of us, including myself, who are influenced more strongly from other cultures. This, you might say, I suppose, from your type of social structures, would be of a sub-structure in a culture.

Our function here is of a studying nature right now, and also observation.

Our form of life has evolved past the usage of wars to settle disputes. We are able to function in this long-range scientific study mode without any particular worry or fear. The other planets can be seen to have craft in the area.

Our culture has been founded in our particular group from the influence of many planets, some of which are in your immediate solar system: Jupiter, Saturn, ancient Mars, current and future Venus, and a more problematical, interdimensional Pluto, though the influences from this outer planet are less stable due to their inter-dimensional existence. More influence from them is felt on the non-physical level.

One may come out to the desert regions to attract craft, especially if you think to the craft, think to the idea that you are willing and able to see and be a part of visionary expeditions and contact. Contact in physical terms may not occur, in fact, is less likely.

Seeking of craft by merely peering up into the sky is also possible, though sightings are more likely to take place in your evening and nighttime hours, when there is less foot traffic on the streets and highways, and also less vehicle traffic. It is not our desire to interrupt your society, and some of our craft may do so in the form of interrupting electrical impulses in your internal combustion engines. We therefore try to limit our closing in on a near pass to your planet to the hours of the early morning, when vehicular traffic is less likely to be in the area.

We welcome you and encourage you to come and be with us at any time you wish to make contact. I have attempted to describe the ship or craft for you so that you may find it easier to make this contact, but if you wish to just make any contact in the area, just think to the area of the desert, and the dark sky, and the stars that are moving. (Brief laugh.) These may not be stars, but are likely to be craft.

In the following sections, Joopah of Zeta Reticuli responds to a number of questions concerning technological developments on earth, his life on his craft, and the role of technology and Liquid Light in his culture and others.

The formal recognition of negative consciousness raising will be picked up, so to speak, by the medical profession, and there will be some effort made to encourage children to believe in wellness rather than the consciousness of dis-ease. It is a beginning.

Current thought in the development of treatment programs will soon be affected by an evolution of consciousness in your medical profession. These programs will be applied toward the eventual goal to foster positive growth.

Question: What type of work is taking place in the scientific community at this time that you care to comment on?

Joopah: There are certain experiments, I will say, in areas in which you may be interested, such as entertainment electronics, which has become an eye-catching source of free-time involvement through the use of video games. But once the attention has been caught, there just might be seen on your horizon more meaningful games to raise the consciousness in a more positive way. They may not be widely accepted at first, but those who will accept them are likely to be influental in the long run, and they are most likely to be children.

As far as areas involving exploring, anthropology, archeology--great influence here, since this type of adventure appeals widely. Archeologists just might be finding a lot of interesting things these days; artifacts from civilizations much advanced to your own. Thought to be ancient civilizations and yet so advanced. Possibly artifacts from your future.

Some research may be done on the floor of the ocean. Perhaps while individuals are looking for other things, they might just find something and take it along and realize later that there is no connection to their current project. They might be piqued to look further by the unusual shapes and, I would say, clear forms of pyramid shapes that can be held in the palm of the hand and may just possibly produce altered states. This type of development will be noticed by crew members on the ship, not by science team members.

It is good to feed the consciousness, though it is ever-changing and evolving. It's good to remind the soul of that which it may confront at any moment it chooses.

Question: How long do you spend on your craft in our terms? Would you spend most of your lifetime on a craft or is it a brief mission, in our terms of time?

Joopah: We do not spend most of our lifetimes anywhere we do not choose to be. But some do make this our life's work, so to speak, though we will return to our, as we say, base craft--or, you may say, mother craft--to resupply and exchange experiences with others of our group. We are not required to spend our lifetimes on these missions, but rather choose to spend, frequently a lifetime, you might say. A lifetime for us would be approximately 227 of your years.

This current mission which I am involved with, as far as the awakening of your planet to this "New Age" as it is called, is a mission which is 50 of your years in duration. We are supplied from our mother craft and will spend most of our time either on a small surveillance craft which we will be in with a crew of four or five, or we will spend our time on the mother craft.

We exist in a rather quiet environment, not just quiet since we communicate telepathically for the most part; the craft itself is very quiet. It makes no particular noise. It is suitable for us since the planet itself is quiet and, you might say, restful. This is a discipline which we have engendered within ourselves, since we have many individuals living on the planet and if we did not have this discipline, so to speak, which comes out of a peace within the entire body, peace of mind you might say, there would be a riot of noise. But due to this peace within ourselves and connections with our whole selves, we do appreciate this quiet and calm atmosphere. This is part of the reason we will use a dull red light and very soft light within the craft. This very soft light is actually quite bright to us, since our eyes are large enough so that they have what you would call light-gathering qualities, such as your optical instruments would be geared toward. Therefore a very small amount of light is quite bright to us.

Social life, as you understand it, on the craft, is a more demure situation, quiet. We do not have great lengthy conversations as you will have here, but rather we are here for our own purpose. We understand our purpose. This is not to say that we are automatons, for we are not. We are tied in, so to speak, to the mass consciousness of the planet, and can share the warmth and unity of that at any time. We do not have to be on the planet, but we are emotionally tied in to that, though emotions are not something that we have in your sense of the word. But there is this relationship, this bond to our own mass consciousness, which gives us the purpose to continue in our task. So our life on the craft, for the most part, is quiet, engaged in our scientific and social work.

Question: Are you able to see us (as, say, non-physical entities like Samuel can) in terms of future selves and future time, or do you see us more as we see ourselves to exist now?

Joopah: We do, for the most part, see you more as you exist in the current, though our ability to tie in to the mass consciousness of the planet can allow us at times to understand your mass consciousness. It is very much as though, to explain in your terms, a trunk (long-distance) call was being made. We tie into our mass consciousness, which ties into your mass consciousness, which filters out your whole self and thence we have an understanding of, in terms of your time, where you have been and where are you going. This is a simplified version of what occurs, but you understand it does not take any delay to occur but it is instantaneous.

Question: If you wanted to take a look at my day-to-day physical life, are you able to do that by telepathic means or do you sometimes use mechanical means for that?

Joopah: Mechanical means are really unnecessary. You see, we are known as a technological culture. This is something, for the most part, we have developed at this time to share with planets such as yours, who are technologically oriented. For in order to awaken your entire planet spiritually at this time, would perhaps be traumatic for some people. It is simpler to make the conversion, spiritually speaking, on a slower basis, and come about to this same place, the same goal, through technological means which we can supply, due to our advanced technocracy. But we, ourselves, do not have an absolute necessity as individuals to use technology. What we do have is vast knowledge in using and incorporating technology within our daily lives and, for that matter, within your lives.

Question: I'm still interested in this Liquid Light technique. It seems to me from what I know, which is very little, that Liquid Light can be utilized for many, many purposes. Is that correct? It could be a creative energy, it could be an energy of being amongst people, a thought-form. Am I correct at least in that?

Joopah: Yes.

Question: What comes closest for us to understand the Liquid Light experience?

Joopah: All right then, for you, understand that when the sun comes up in the morning the sun is really Liquid Light. You all on this planet cooperate in allowing that sun to be present. It is a conscious cooperation, and you will remind yourself that it is a conscious event when you will eclipse the sun. Even though you are not really aware of consciously doing this, it is a way to show you, as you will show yourself, that you really are in charge of your reality. The sun, as all suns are, is really Liquid Light. You perceive that the sun gives forth rays which cause creative effects, help the plants to grow and so on. And yet in truth, the sun in its own right causes plants to exist. You will give your power, in this sense, to the sun and allow it to take credit for growth in creatures, consciousness and plants. For if you think about it, you will understand that plants have consciousness also.

This idea of the sun as Liquid Light is really about as close as you can understand right now to an event which happens normally within your everyday society.

Question: The liquid analogy being then what we would call being bathed in the sunlight? In a sense it bathes everything it reaches almost like a liquid.

Joopah: You will feel a renewal of your life energies by, as you say, taking a sun bath. It is really that light is only a representation of energy, and as such it is energy in its purest form. So you will take an energy bath, but you will also create that source of energy. So you will create the source and absorb from it. You will be a part of the creation and participation. So really, it is quite similar to what we do in our theater. We will create an image and participate together to create this image manufactured out of white light or energy (Figure 8). It is very similar to what you will do when you take a sun bath.

Question: I'm curious about the potentials of using white light for various art forms other than this theater that you speak of, for visual arts, sculptures, two-dimensional and four-dimensional pieces of art. Can you go into any detail?

Figure 8

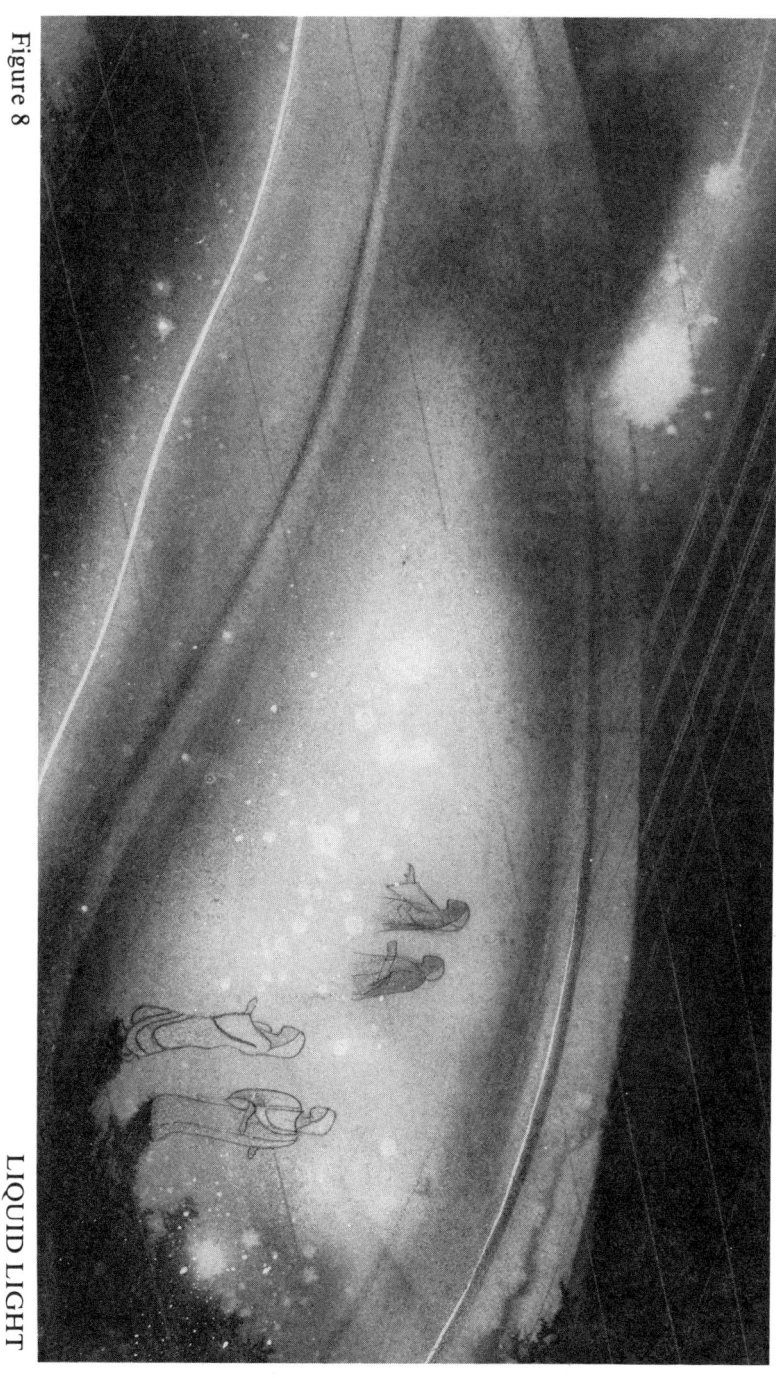

LIQUID LIGHT

Joopah: It will be commonly used in other cultures, better explained by them, for seemingly four-dimensional sculptures which will float in the air, as it will seem. They can be touched and will move about, tumble, and return to their original location. When they are touched, they will take on the colors and the tones of the individual touching them.

They will put forth musical sounds which will correspond to the vibrations within that individual.

For individuals who believe in discomfort, tones will be unpleasant. For individuals who believe in bodily integrity, the tones will be pleasant and constant.

So sculptures will not only perform acts of beauty and spiritual upliftment, but also a service to the individual. A way, you might say, of checking up on how you are feeling, really what you are feeling.

They will, in this sense, be again harmonically balanced to the musical scale of the individual participant who comes in contact with them.

Question: Joopah, I'm curious about the people who participate in creating these four-dimensional sculptures. Are there certain people who are artists, or do all people participate in this?

Joopah: Just as you will choose in your lives to explore certain facets of experience, so individuals will do so elsewhere also. There are, then, you might say, artisans-- an artisan class which will produce, out of pure joy, elements of their experience, utilizing the highest forms of personal interrelated technology, which can activate and deactivate itself automatically when brought into contact with individuals. They will then utilize, you might say in your vernacular, the latest technology in order to keep up with the idea that people will wish to interact with art, be a part of it. It is not enough, really, to be just an onlooker.

In order to feel a part of any event, one needs to be involved. It is similar to your old fashioned movie, where the bouncing ball will go from word to word and the audience will sing. In order to be a part of an event, individuals must feel they are more than just an onlooker. They must truly feel that their participation is necessary for the completion of the event to their satisfaction.

Question: I'm curious about the actual way these works are created, as in our world, for example, I will take a brush with paint or I will take fabric and stitch, do whatever the technical aspects require. How are these works technically executed?

Joopah: You are asking how Liquid Light is formed into an image. We will, and those who choose to participate, form thought first. An image, you might say, in your mind's eye, of what form the sculpture should take. Then, utilizing Liquid Light technology, just like the creation of the bird, the form is created in air. In order to produce tones, lights, colors within it, it is only necessary to ground that thought. Now we do not run a wire into the ground. The thought is grounded in that the artisan who develops, produces the sculpture will really, in a way for you to understand, leave a little bit of his own consciousness with each sculpture. He will choose to allow colors, allow tones, will truly leave a part of his own consciousness within this sculpture. Thus the sculpture becomes not just a machine, not just an image of living light, but a true form of the extended consciousness of this artist.

When participants touch the sculpture, in that sense, they will be touching the artist also. It will be that the artist will be aware when harmonious balances are created around and through the sculpture. The artist will be enriched, you might say, charged up by the exchange between the sculpture and the participants, you would say onlookers, who touch the sculpture. It is a way of mutually enhancing each others' dynamics. This form of art does not exist in my system as it is not our choice, but it is common in other worlds.

The Rite, or ceremony, that Joopah describes in what follows is a form of theatrical production on his planet. The event was experienced by a person from Earth whom we shall refer to as "Anderson." The memories of this journey were not consciously available to Anderson, but were discovered by documented hypnotic investigation later.

When individuals from our planet are taken aboard craft and journey to other worlds, it is common for them not to have a conscious recollection of the experience. Usually the memories will slowly begin to return, often in dream states, and eventually the full memory will return. Hypnosis allows a full recollection of the experience to be retained consciously, and this was the case with Anderson, who is now consciously aware of the event.

Anderson remembers being escorted into a large, open area, or arena, under a dome-like structure. A large, eagle-like bird appeared. From behind the bird there appeared to be a source of a very bright and intense white light.

As Anderson watched, the bird went up in flames, seemingly as a result of the light, and was reduced to a pile of ashes. From these ashes appeared a caterpillar-like creature which represented a new beginning, life being born from the ashes.

Anderson was very moved by this experience, and attributed to the event many religious associations.

Now the individual in question, Anderson, was brought forth to the planet in order to participate in, what you might say, Annual Rite of Renewal.

The idea was to join with the group present in theater to form an alliance in cultural thought.

The giant bird is a symbol of technique, really a symbol of creative flight of thought.

The association with light does not cause discomfort to this holographic image of a bird. It is truly a thought-form, Liquid Light phenomenon, wherein the thought-form of this bird transforms into a beginning. Heat and light used as a catalyst to bring forth a new beginning. The bird seems to melt down into a small pile of ashes. The symbol being that a new bird or flight of thought would take place from that point on, and become the symbol for a new beginning.

It is really an honor to be present.

Dignitaries and ambassadors from other systems are brought into this arena, or theater as you would say, to observe this Rite of Renewal. The idea of a flight symbol, the bird, is quite universal on systems influenced by Zeta Reticuli culture. The bird is used as symbol of creative thought. This is a universal symbol of all cultures, all planets we have traveled to. The bird is recognized, if not just in thought, then in sensation. What the bird is about is perceived by inhabitants of planets we have contacted.

Question: Is this where our planet's legend of the Phoenix originates?

Joopah: It is really a universal symbol, strictly speaking. Universe-universal symbol. It is a thought which runs through cultures. It is, then, the core of that Phoenix idea. We choose to participate in this act of the rebirth of thought when changes are taking place which will be positive. This is why Anderson was honored in this fashion, though we understood that at the time, she was less than aware consciously of what the ceremony was all about. But in time, telepathically, she will understand. It will be explained.

Question: Then as an Annual Rite, is this something that is performed on a regular basis on the planet for invited guests?

Joopah: Dignitaries, you might say, yes. When individuals are invited to attend, such as Anderson, it is with the knowledge, forethought you might say, that Anderson would put forth her experience. So in this sense, she was an Ambassador dignitary.

Question: What kinds of things did the Rite itself consist of?

Joopah: Well, there is a large space. The room appears to be a dome from the inside. There is space for our citizens to stand, in what you would call audience, but they are not onlookers, they are participants. For it is the participants within who create the light. They literally create the thought-form which is represented in the shape of the bird, about 50 feet in height, about 35 feet in width. Participants will bring forth this thought-form. You understand that thoughts on your planet will take form as every place else. A tree is first a thought, and then takes shape in form. We are aware of this process and are willing to participate in the actual event.

So the bird is brought forth out of the consciousness of the participants, who are disciplined in thought so that they concentrate totally on the event as it should take place for the dignitary. Their minds never waver from the event of the bird on the stage looking birdlike, not unusual. Then the light appears from behind the bird. There is white light and heat. A sensation of heat can be produced, but is not vital for the event. It was produced for Anderson, since it was felt she would

75

appreciate the idea of light as the sun. Warmth, positive image, not just bright light. For some dignitaries, heat is not necessary.

The light itself does not reduce the bird to ashes. It is the thought. It is very much a participatory theatrical act in which all participants present, except the dignitaries usually, will focus their complete attention on directing this performance, though it is a reality, a true event. In complete depth a holographic image is not transparent, translucent, it is solid and yet light densities and properties of the bird are somewhat liquid. The bird is then reduced to ashes in the sense that your physical bodies, when you pass out of them, will reduce themselves to dust.

From that dust, if allowed to mix with other elements naturally, will come other life, continuing the species and cooperating harmonically with all other species. This theater is a representation of that harmony.

Question: Would this be representative, then, of what we would call theater on your planet, or is this something that is done only for outside Ambassadors?

Joopah: It is a special occasion. Theatrical events on our planet are not as on yours. They involve individuals getting together in groups, such as these participants for this theatrical event, and learning to focus their attention for a length of time to produce effects such as those stated before. The idea being to train for universal harmony between them. The participants form a bond between them, united in their cause of creating this event. It is a way we will come together and join harmonically.

Question: The creation of that universal harmony--can that be utilized by those same individuals for another purpose?

Joopah: It is possible to form objects when they are needed out of elements which are present at any given point in the universe. You would say, forming objects out of thin air, but really, air contains many elements in suspension. Objects can by synthesized out of available sources.

Question: Would the bird be a type that we would recognize, such as an eagle? I believe that is how Anderson described it.

Joopah: Looks very much like that sort of bird, yes.

Question: Will the light that is created have hue in the same way that our light does?

Joopah: It is white light.

Question: But it doesn't come from a source, such as we would think of a light source, right?

Joopah: It is created by the participants focusing their energy within a focal point. It is a form of Liquid Light technology, which, in the final analysis, is the ultimate technology within that framework. Many craft which function in other dimensions will utilize this technology exclusively for their travels. Liquid Light thought-form vehicles are very difficult for your technology to detect.

Question: Were musical tones involved in this theater Rite?

Joopah: No audible tone is heard.

Question: Are tones used on your planet in what we would consider a musical form?

Joopah: Not in the form you would understand as music. For us, we consider constant and similar vibrations between individuals as proper harmonic balance amongst the civilization. It is adequate for our needs and we are comfortable with serving our needs and serving in general in the universe.

Question: That inaudible tone, then, used by the participants or actors in creating the bird formation, is that one tone which they all share?

Joopah: Yes. It is a moment of complete pure tone,

which is identical from individual to individual. If you could blow a note on a tuning instrument and make that note pure, crisp and clear, then that note would be just as pure, crisp and clear in vibration from participant to participant. They will all need to be completely in tune with each other in order to perform this act, which is symbolic of all creation.

Question: Within that singular tone, are there complementary pitches?

Joopah: No. It is a singular tone.

Question: Would this event, then, represent the Song of Creation?

Joopah: Yes. It is, on this planetary system, our form of what you will do in dance of creation which you will call "making love." Our form of birthing does not require that act.

Question: So this would represent for the individual participants the same significance, in terms of emotional fulfillment--to emotionally connect with their part in the creation process?

Joopah: Yes. It is a way of uniting with other citizens in a union of knowledgeable forethought. It will be necessary to think ahead while you are creating objects out of light, and yet you must focus your attention in the moment. It requires, then, the ability to think and act simultaneously.

CONCLUSION BY SAMUEL

Now that you have completed your reading of this volume one, you will truly notice, those of you who have paid attention, that you are feeling a little different about yourself. You are perhaps visualizing events that don't seem to make sense in your present circumstances.

You will find that, in the future set of circumstances you will create for you, that your events will be right down that path of creative joy which is right for you.

In time, you will all be a part of these concepts which have been presented to you. You will, if you choose, be involved with these off-planet beings. Some of you can meet them, be with them. Some of you can meet them, be with them. Some of you will choose to sort of blaze a path for them and for you, by talking to your friends, by really involving yourself in the thoughtful awareness which will be a part of your becoming. You will then really not be a reader but a true participant in the coming change of awareness. Which will allow your planet, Earth as you now call it (perhaps some of you would like to refer to it as Terra), positive changes which will truly benefit all of mankind.

So then you will find, interspersed among your friends and allies, those beings who will truly help you to become all that you can be. The magnificent beings among you are you yourselves. Those of you who read this material and assimilate it into the proper sequence of events for you will find that your introduction to these beliefs will only allow you to really create your own beautiful planet of awareness within you, and as you go along, you will be able to allow the creation of that planet without you--that is, out beyond your own personal physical perimeters.

You will, upon creating that inner joy, be able to

influence others in many joyful ways. Positively allowing them to be that wonderful, magnificent being they can all be, as you are.

So in time, know that for you this is not a volume, but really a key to your own destiny. A key which will unlock those thoughts and beliefs which will allow the future creative forces to spread out upon the land of your beloved Terra, and begin that work which will allow your planet to be that beautiful place, as it is described in the thoughts and memories which you will have when reading this material.

Know that in the coming volumes you will find more intriguing memories within you as you read this, for you are truly participants. Not participants in an experiment by others, but participants in a lesson you have created for yourselves. This book, then, is really only one of many keys upon a chain which you yourselves wear. It is truly one of the keys to your future destiny. You can truly unlock those locks you have placed upon your own chains. You need not wear those chains any longer, but can truly be all that you are.

In the future for you, then, know that there will be many friends and compadres for you, and all will proceed upon these lines lovingly and in harmony with all others. There is no need for any negative thoughts. Don't feel the need to argue with anyone about this material. For those of you who understand the true nature of this key, arguing will only contradict the whole message.

For you, then, know that when those memories are jarred, when those good feelings flood into you, then you will know that you have truly found your own inner key, your own inner awareness, which will allow you to flower and be that truly magnificent being that you all really are.

--Samuel